3.50

BLACK MOUNTAIN BOY

A Story of the Boyhood

of John Honie

Written
by
Vada Carlson
and
Gary Witherspoon

Illustrated
by
Andy Tsinajinnie

Published
by the
NAVAJO CURRICULUM CENTER PRESS
PHOENIX, ARIZONA

1974

REVISED EDITION
© 1974 Schoolboard, Inc.
Rough Rock, Arizona
All rights reserved.

International Standard Book Number: 0-89019-008-9
Library of Congress Catalog Card Number: 68-27160

Manufactured in the United States of America

**O'SULLIVAN
WOODSIDE
& COMPANY**
2218 East Magnolia
Phoenix, Arizona 85034

Table of Contents

FOREWORD

Black Mountain Boy is a book which has been prepared primarily for Navaho boys and girls. However, we firmly believe it can contribute toward a broader understanding among all people and can be used successfully with non-Navaho students. This book is one of a series which attempts to present materials related to Navaho life and culture.

It is our belief that Navaho youth should have the opportunity to learn about themselves and their culture as do other American children in other schools.

The Rough Rock Demonstration School, among its many areas of endeavor, is dedicated to the preparation of books and other classroom materials which can be used in schools throughout this region. We believe that in this manner we can help Navaho children achieve a positive self-image. No one can foretell the future, but everyone knows that tomorrow will be different from today. It is our firm conviction that we must give to our youth today the tools with which to make intelligent choices tomorrow. In this way, and in this way only, can Navaho students take their places and be contributing citizens in the world of the future.

We are proud to offer this book as a contribution toward a better life for Navaho youth.

BOARD OF EDUCATION
ROUGH ROCK DEMONSTRATION SCHOOL

TEDDY McCURTAIN, *President*
YAZZIE BEGAY, *Vice President*
JOHN DICK, *Member*
ASHIE TSOSIE, *Member*
BENJAMIN WOODY, *Member*
WHITEHAIR'S SON, *Member*
THOMAS JAMES, *Member*

PREFACE

This book, *Black Mountain Boy,* is one of a series being developed by the Navaho Curriculum Center, Rough Rock Demonstration School, Rough Rock, Arizona. The community at Rough Rock, through the School Board, has requested books which discuss subjects and incidents of historical and personal interest that occurred in the Rough Rock area, on and near Black Mountain and on the Navaho Reservation in general.

It is hoped that *Black Mountain Boy,* together with the other works of the series, will add significantly to the education and understanding of children presently enrolled at Rough Rock and, furthermore, be very useful in other schools located both on and off the reservation.

One of the principles underlying positive education is the necessity for each individual child to feel a sense of worth, not only in himself and in his family, but in his community and nation. While schools on Indian reservations usually have units in the lower primary grades dealing with the family and community, I am unaware of any actual published materials which bring together basic history, biographies and other important information dealing with a particular locale and its people.

The purpose of the publications developed by the Navaho Curriculum Center at the Rough Rock Demonstration School is to provide Navaho youth with the same opportunities in education that are provided other American citizens. It is a well known fact that schools and libraries throughout this nation are full of books dealing with the "average American." Usually these books depict blond-haired, blue-eyed children running to meet their father when he comes from work. Perhaps these books are effective in promoting the self-image and positive sense of identification for the middle class blond-haired and blue-eyed individuals reading them. We have no quarrel with their effectiveness for those people, but we have strenuous and vigorous reservations about the books and their usefulness and appropriateness in Indian education.

It also is a well known fact that the American Indians, in the past, have been denied an opportunity in school to read and learn about themselves in a positive and meaningful manner. The Rough Rock Demonstration School, aware of this problem, as has been Indian education for decades, has embarked upon an extensive program of designing, developing and preparing books and other materials dealing with Navaho life, history, biographies, current programs, etc.

The Demonstration School believes completely that Indian youths in the past have been denied an equal and proper education because of the inadequacy and inappropriateness of the materials and books used.

Dr. Karl Menninger, perhaps the world's most renowned psychiatrist, long has lamented the fact that Indian education has neglected the fundamental cornerstone on which all education should be based. He believes that Indian education has neglected the Indian child and has made him consciously or unconsciously ashamed of who he is and, therefore, unable to meet the changing world with confidence. Dr. Menninger feels that Indian education should exert every effort to assist the Indian child in being proud of his past and confident of his future.

Without a positive self-image and this positive sense of identification, no person, regardless of nationality or background, can achieve his full potential. It is hoped that this book, with other volumes in the series, will trigger throughout the reservations in this nation comparable efforts to prepare materials dealing with the life and culture of our Indian Americans.

ROBERT A. ROESSEL, JR., *Director*
Rough Rock Demonstration School

4

INTRODUCTION

Black Mountain Boy is the story of a Navaho boy who grew up on Black Mountain during the early part of the Twentieth Century. Black Mountain is in the northeastern corner of Arizona on the Navaho reservation. It is near the geographical center of the reservation just northwest of Chinle.

John Honie is the boy around whom the story is centered. The events of the book occurred when John was five to sixteen years old. At the time of publication (1968) John still is living on Black Mountain and is a highly respected medicine man.

John Honie's maternal grandparents lived near Grey Mountain, which is just north of the San Francisco Peaks and Flagstaff, Arizona. John's maternal grandmother (bimá sání) was called The Daughter of the Man with Curly Hair (Hastiin Bitsii' Yisch'ilí Bitsi') and was of the "Yucca Fruit Drawn Out in a Line People" clan (Hask'-aan Hadzohí). John's maternal grandfather (bicheii) was called Bitter Water (Tó'dích'íiní) and was, as the name suggests, of the "Bitter Water" clan. John's maternal grandparents were living at Grey Mountain when they were forced, like other Navahos, to make the long walk to Fort Sumner, New Mexico.

John's mother (Yił Hanazbaa') was a young girl around eight years of age when she and her family made the trip to Fort Sumner. She had a younger brother (Haské' Yik'-ehgo'ííyá) who also made the trip.

Upon their return from Fort Sumner, John's mother's family spent a year at Fort Defiance under the control of the U. S. Cavalry and Indian Department officials. In the spring of 1870 John's mother and her mother, grandparents, and maternal uncles moved to Lukachukai where they lived for about five years.

One of John's maternal grandmother's brothers, Black Whiskers (Dághaa' Diłhiłi), married a daughter of Big Man's Brother (Hastiin Tso Bik'is). Big Man's Brother was from Black Mountain and had refused to go to Fort Sumner. He had escaped from the cavalry while hiding on Black Mountain. Because he had large herds of cattle, sheep and goats, Big Man's Brother invited Black Whiskers to bring all of his family from Lukachukai to Black Mountain.

At that time (1880) very few people lived on Black Mountain, although the land was beautiful and the grass plentiful. So John's mother and her relatives moved to Black Mountain with their livestock.

Shortly after their arrival on Black Mountain, John's mother was married to John's father. John's father was a son of Big Man's Brother. John's parents had lived together in harmony for just over 50 years when John's father died in 1938. His mother passed away in 1954. John's parents had ten children, of whom John was the ninth. Another central character in the story, Big Sister, was the third child of John's parents.

John grew up in the beauty, abundance and seclusion of Black Mountain. When he was a young boy, people on Black Mountain had large numbers of livestock. John recalls that his parents had more than 200 head of cattle and over 2,000 sheep and goats. These large flocks required a great deal of care and work. Every able-bodied person in the family and extended family worked with the livestock. Navaho children were taught to be good shepherds at very young ages. John was five years old when he started herding the sheep with his older sister.

The story focuses on John's boyhood and on his relationship with his older sister, affectionately called Big Sister in the story. The story is full of dramatic and charming experiences, and should be delightful and educational reading for both student and teacher.

ACKNOWLEDGMENTS

In acknowledging the work done on this book, principal thanks go to John Honie who very generously made available many of his intimate experiences and feelings as a boy. Della Jumbo and Paul Platero translated the tape recordings from which the book was written. Vada Carlson prepared the original draft. After extensive research and several long days of consultation with John Honie, I revised and rewrote the text. Andy Tsinajinnie did the excellent illustrations which accompany and virtually are a part of the story. Broderick H. Johnson edited the manuscript and supervised the book through its publication stages.

Appreciation also is expressed to the Board of Directors of D.I.N.É., Inc. (Allen D. Yazzie, Ned Hatathli and Guy Gorman), to the Rough Rock Board of Education and to the administration of the Rough Rock Demonstration School (Robert A. Roessel, Jr., Director; Dillon Platero, Deputy Director, and Anita Pfeiffer, Assistant Director for Educational Services) for the foresight and vision that they displayed in implementing the Navaho Curriculum Center and guiding it successfully.

Funds for the operation of the Navaho Curriculum Center came from grants by the Office of Economic Opportunity and by Public Law 89-10, Title I, received through the United States Bureau of Indian Affairs.

GARY WITHERSPOON, *Director*
Navaho Curriculum Center

John Honie is a highly respected Navaho medicine man who knows and performs seven ceremonies: Lifeway, Beautyway, Ghostway, Red and White Antway, Windway and Male Shootingway. He was born October 15, 1901, at his mother's home on Black Mountain. He is a member of the "Yucca Fruit Drawn Out in a Line" clan (Hask'aan Hadzohí) which originated from the Ta'neeszahníí clan. He was born for the "Mexican" clan (Nakaii Diné'é)*. John and his wife, Margaret, have seven children, sixteen grandchildren and one great grandchild. The family resides on Black Mountain at a place called "Where the Wind Blows Around the Rock" (Tsé Binááyołi).

*Father's clan

Chapter One

Big Sister and Learning to Herd the Sheep

It was springtime in Navaholand and Honie, the little Navaho boy, was happy. The mountain air was cold, but the sunshine was warm. Already there were two tiny lambs in the herd of sheep.

Honie felt big that morning. He was just five years old, but Big Sister had asked him to go with her. He would help her and the two dogs herd the sheep.

"Go slowly, Little Brother," Big Sister called to him, as he ran with the black dog to turn two of the ewes back into the herd. "There is no hurry. Our sheep would as soon graze here as anywhere on the mountain. You'll be tired soon enough."

Honie stopped running. He walked beside Big Sister for a little way; then he saw a high ridge nearby. He ran over to it and began climbing.

From the top he looked down at the sheep, the dogs and Big Sister. Everything looked different. He could see far down the mountain trail. He had been down there one time. He had gone with his father and mother to the very foot of the mountain. There was a little store there that had just been built. They had traded a rug for some supplies which they had strapped onto the pack horse his father led.

He remembered the ride back up the steep trail. He had clung to his mother, afraid he'd slip off the horse trail.

His thoughts were interrupted by Big Sister. She motioned for him to come down from the high ridge.

Honie took one more look. The sheep looked very small. The dogs were almost as small as prairie dogs. Big Sister looked no larger than Little Sister who was just learning to toddle around the hogan. The view made him feel bigger than ever.

The sheep were moving from the little clearing into the forest of pine and piñon. Suddenly Big Sister disappeared from sight.

Honie felt like a small boy again. Suppose Big Sister left him behind and he couldn't find her?

He scrambled down from the ridge, taking care not to slip and fall. It seemed a long way down, much farther than it had seemed as he climbed up.

When he caught up with Big Sister he was puffing and panting. His cheeks were as red as his headband and his eyes were bright with excitement.

Big Sister smiled at him.

"You climbed to the very top," she said. "What did you see?"

11

He tried to tell her.

"The sheep looked only so big," he said, measuring with his hands. "The whole world was different. I could see far down the trail. Even you were little."

Big Sister nodded.

"That's the way it is," she agreed. "You will see many wonderful things, now that you are big enough to help me with the sheep . . . . I think more baby lambs will be born today. You must watch the mothers for me. We must not leave them behind with their lambs."

"Why? Would they wander off and be lost?" Honie asked.

"Yes, or some animal might kill a lamb and carry it off."

Honie's eyes grew round with worry. He looked behind him, then to right and left.

"I don't see any bad animals," he said.

"No, they hide from us," Big Sister said. "But **they** see **us.**"

Honie moved closer to his sister. He spoke softly so that any animals that might be watching could not hear him. "Where do they hide?"

"Oh, in the rocks. Behind trees. In clumps of bushes," Big Sister said. "Sometimes an eagle swoops down and carries off a lamb. There are two up there now."

Honie looked up. Two huge birds soared far up in the blue sky, perhaps watching the herd and the herders.

Just then the black dog began acting strangely. He growled low in his throat and started toward a thick stand of timber.

12

Honie was a little afraid.

"Does he see something bad?" he whispered, afraid to name the animal he feared the dog might have smelled or seen.

Big Sister stood very still, looking about her. Then she called the dog back.

It's only a doe, with a tiny spotted fawn," she told Honie. "Look to your right. In the thicket. She will slip away. She's afraid of us and the dogs. Do you see her?"

The doe moved. The fawn followed beside it like a shadow. Honie had never seen anything more beautiful. The

scene was one of peace. The sheep grazed. The dogs watched. The doe and the fawn disappeared into the forest.

He could not put his feeling into words, but he knew all was beauty, and he, Honie, was a part of that beauty.

"Yes," he said. "I saw her. It is good to know there are many good and beautiful things."

As the hours sped past, the sun shone brightly and Honie felt tired. He sat down beside a fallen tree, and, leaning against it, he put his head on one arm and went to sleep.

When he woke he looked at once for his sister. She stood quietly among the grazing sheep.

Then he heard a soft crying sound nearby and saw a newborn lamb struggling to get to its feet. Its mother stood a little distance away, looking at it as though she were afraid of it.

Honie jumped up and ran to help the baby lamb. The mother sheep stamped her foot, but he paid no attention to her. With his back to the angry ewe, he bent over the lamb.

At once something hit him on the seat of his pants, and

he fell on the other side of the struggling lamb. When he tried to get up, the ewe lowered her head and hit him again.

This time he sat very still. The lamb struggled to its feet. The ewe went to it. She sniffed at it and began nudging it. Suddenly the lamb found her warm udder and began nursing.

When the lamb had its fill, the mother walked away and the lamb followed her.

Honie got up. He felt the seat of his pants. He wanted to cry, but he was too big to cry. He rubbed the spot, then carefully walked away.

"That sheep was mad at me," he told his sister. "I was just trying to help her baby when she bumped me. She bumped me twice. Here!" Honie said, patting the place.

His sister laughed.

"You have much to learn, Little Brother," she told him. "You have much to learn about herding sheep, and there are other things you must learn, also."

"What?" Honie asked.

"You must learn about plants and the clouds and water. You must learn about sunshine and cold. You must learn about snow and rain."

"I like to watch the rainbows," Honie said.

"I like to watch the rainbows, too," Big Sister replied, "but always we must watch the sheep. The sheep give us everything."

"They give us wool for our mother's rugmaking." Honie said.

"And food," Big Sister reminded him. "What would we do without our mutton stew and our mutton roasts. I think we would be hungry without our sheep."

16

"And cold," Honie added. "I like to sleep on my sheep-skins and roll up in my rugs and blankets at night. The wool is soft and the covers are warm. I sleep well."

The black dog and the brown dog both barked loudly. They had something cornered and they were jumping and snapping at it.

"They've found something. I wonder what it is. Maybe it's a bear," Honie cried, running toward them.

"Wait! Move cautiously," Big Sister warned. "It's not a bear, but it may be a skunk or a porcupine."

As they walked nearer they saw it was a badger, in the door of his den.

"It's just Old Man Badger," Big Sister laughed. "I don't think they'll risk being slapped by his sharp claws." She called to the dogs. "Come on, foolish fellows. Get back to work. You don't need badger meat for lunch. Go herd the sheep."

The dogs left the badger and came running up to Honie and his sister, their red tongues hanging out and their tails wagging.

"They were having fun," Honie said. "They were teasing Old Man Badger."

"Work dogs are for working, and herders are for herding," Big Sister said. "And here is something you must learn. The dogs are smart and they will help you, but you must know how to tell them what to do. Watch me." With waves of her hand she sent one dog around the herd to the right and the other to the left.

When Honie and his sister drove the herd back to the corral that night there were twelve lambs, instead of the two they had driven out in the morning.

18

Honie felt proud of himself. He had helped with the lambing. He soon would be able to herd sheep all by himself.

"Can I stay with you in the corral tonight?" he asked Big Sister.

"I think you will need to sleep where it is warm," she said. "Sometimes it gets very cold in the corral, and sometimes — ," she looked all around to be sure no one else heard her — "sometimes I am afraid . . . . I hear things. I wonder what I would do if something tried to slip through the dark and steal some of our beautiful lambs."

"If I had a bow and some arrows, like Tall Man has," Honie said, "or a gun, like my father has, I'd shoot anything that tried to eat my sheep."

Big Sister put one hand on his shoulder.

"Soon enough, Little Brother, you will be doing a man's work," she said. "Tonight, sleep. I will have a pile of rocks near me, and a little fire. And our father has promised to help, now that the lambs are coming."

The sheep were tired and full of new green grass. They went willingly to the corral.

Many Navahos had corrals like those into which he and his sister drove their sheep that late afternoon in the spring. There was a jutting ledge of rock, scooped out by the wind to make a cave-like shelter. Across the front of it, Honie's father and older brothers had built a strong wall of rocks. The gateway was made of poles. When the sheep relaxed and bedded down close together, it was warm in the back part of the corral which kept the desert winds from striking the sleeping sheep with force.

"Now we will eat," said Big Sister.

Honie felt his stomach. It was flat. He was tired and hungry and thirsty, but he was happy. He had herded the sheep all day with his sister. He loved his sister. She scolded

him sometimes, but not often. She wanted him to be a good boy, and Honie wanted to be a good boy, so he was not angry with her for correcting him.

Their mother had food ready for them when they reached the hogan. Honie ate, then lay down on his sheep-skin and went to sleep.

It seemed only minutes until his Big Sister was shaking him awake.

"Are you going to be a little boy and stay in the hogan with your mother," she asked him, "or will you be a big boy and go with me to herd the sheep?"

"I will go with you," he said.

It was every bit as beautiful that morning as it had been the day before. Perhaps it was more beautiful, for there were fluffy clouds in the blue sky, and a gentle breeze stirred the branches of the trees and waved the young grass.

Big Sister looked at the sky.

"I think it may rain today," she said. "We will not take the sheep far from home."

Honie looked at the sky. He wondered why his sister thought it might rain. He saw no signs of it.

Because of the many lambs in the flock, the sheep moved slowly. There had been twelve last night. Now there were twice that many. There was one black lamb. It had a cute face, partly white, and a mass of curls on its forehead.

"It's a nice lamb," Big Sister said. "I like to have a few black ones in the flock. They are so easy to see at a distance."

By noon the fluffy clouds had piled up and darkened. The wind blew harder and harder. Dust swirled.

"Let's turn the herd homeward," Big Sister called. "A storm is coming."

Honie rubbed his eyes. They were gritty with dust. He could taste it in his mouth and feel it between his teeth.

The wind was blowing from the direction of their home. The sheep didn't like to face it.

"Hurry!" Big Sister called. "Move them up. We'll get them to the canyon, where they can find shelter. She was walking fast, her skirts blowing. "We must not let Wind be the herder; he'd blow our sheep away," she said.

The air suddenly got colder. The lambs cried for their mothers, and the mothers called back anxiously.

"Are they afraid?" Honie yelled.

"They are worried," Big Sister said. "They know a storm is coming and they want to protect their babies, just as our mother would want to protect your younger sister and you. But we must help the sheep. We must not let them run in fright."

The rain came, in sprinkles at first, then in a pounding downpour.

After reaching the canyon, Honie and Big Sister crawled into the shelter of a low-growing cedar and huddled together, just as the sheep were huddling together in the canyon.

The rain turned to sleet and then to snow. Honie and his sister no longer could see the sheep. They were hidden behind a wall of white feathers of snow. But through the wall they could hear the sheep and lambs calling to each other.

"We must get them home," Big Sister said. "It could be we are going to have a deep snow. Lambs born in it might get sick and die. Come, Little Brother, but stay close to me. I don't want you to get lost in the storm."

Honie never had been out alone in a heavy snowfall. He didn't want to get lost in the cold. He held tightly to Big Sister's wet skirts as they and the loyal dogs began to drive the sheep toward the safety of the corral.

They were both soaking wet from head to foot when they heard a call.

"It's our father and Redhair," Big Sister said. "They've come to help us." (Redhair was Big Sister's husband.)

She called back and soon two dark figures appeared through the snow.

"Take your brother and go home," their father shouted. "We will put the sheep in the corral."

Honie took his sister's hand and ran with her to the shelter of the hogan.

Their mother had a good fire blazing in the center of the hogan. The herders dried themselves and their wet clothing by the fire.

When his teeth stopped chattering from the chill, Honie looked at Big Sister and smiled, "That was fun," he said. "We fought that old storm, didn't we?"

23

"Yes, but I'm glad our father and Redhair came to help us."

Honie looked at his sister. She was drying her long hair which she had loosened from its string-tied bun. He could not see her face.

Big Sister was a good girl. He would be very lonely if she ever left him. Honie ate some food and then went to sleep on his sheepskin.

Chapter Two

Mother's Brother Visits and Tells Stories

(Two Years Later)

"Who is coming?"

Big Sister had heard a sound that told her a horseman was approaching on the mountain trail.

Honie raced to the nearest pile of rocks and scampered up them like a squirrel. From the top he could see half-way down the trail. A man was coming up. He rode an old gray horse.

"It is mother's brother, Tall Man," Honie said. "He is riding his horse that looks like a cloud in the sky."

"Is no one else coming?" she asked.

Honie looked again.

"I do not see anyone else," he reported. "May I run to meet him?"

"Can you go to the trail without getting lost?" Big Sister asked.

"I am getting bigger and bigger," Honie told her. "I'm not a little boy any more."

"Then go," his sister said. "But watch for snakes. They will be coming out of their underground homes, now that the weather is getting warmer."

Honie ran. His legs were strong, after herding sheep with his sister for the last two years. He was taller, too, and he no longer had baby fat on his body.

"Who is running down the trail?" Tall Man asked, pretending to be frightened. "Can this be my sister's son who was on the cradleboard a little time ago?"

"It has been a long time since you visited us," Honie said. "I have grown since then. I am seven years old now. I help Big Sister with the sheep."

"Then you are big enough to ride behind me," Tall Man said, looking pleased with his young nephew (bida'). He leaned over and reached for Honie's hand. "Come on, scramble up behind me."

Honie took his uncle's (bida'i) hand, put one foot on the stirrups and swung himself onto the gray horse, which was very gentle.

"I have brought you a gift," Tall Man said. "I thought you might be well grown. Shall I tell you what it is?"

Honie could see what his uncle held in one hand.

"Is it a bow and arrow?" he asked. "One time you told me you'd make me a good bow."

"How did you guess it?" the uncle smiled. "Here. Take them. I'm tired of carrying them."

"Will you teach me to shoot the arrow?" Honie asked.

"I will teach you," Tall Man said. "That is what mother's brothers are for. And grandparents. Their task is to teach the young ones all the things the parents have no time to teach them. But since your grandfather has passed away, I will have to do most of the teaching. Like shooting with a bow and arrow, and teaching you to tell medicine herbs from ordinary weeds."

28

"And to tell stories," Honie said, looking with pride at the new bow, so neatly made of good wood and wound with sinew. "Will you tell me stories tonight?"

"I will tell you stories until you go to sleep," Tall Man chuckled. "Usually, that is not a very long time."

After they entered the home and had eaten their evening meal, Tall Man sat down in front of the hogan. He spoke to Honie: "It is now time for a story. Sit beside me. I do not want to make my voice loud. A story is best told in a quiet way . . . . That is good."

"Once, a long time ago, a man went out hunting. He was a good hunter, but this time a snowstorm blew up. He could not get home, so he sat down beneath a pine tree. He was very cold.

"Suddenly he heard the voice of a holy person speaking to him out of the storm.

" 'What are you doing here?' the voice asked. The hunter said he had been hunting and that he was very cold. He asked if there was a warm place for him.

"The holy person pointed to a place and the hunter started to go there. As he got near the door he saw a rainbow, and the door was open for him to go inside. Some bears were there. The hunter was cold; so he started a fire, but the bears said, 'We do not want a fire here. Put it out!' So he put the fire out. Then the bears said, 'Go outside, while we put on our good clothes.' So he went outside. When they finished dressing, they told the man to come back inside.

"He slept with the bears that night and stayed warm. The holy person told the bears that human beings can offer pollen and prayers toward the bear tracks. The hunter also learned some prayers and sacred songs while he was with the bears.

"There are many kinds of bears, just as there are many kinds of people. No one knows what clan this hunter belonged to, or where he was born, or where he lived.

"When morning came he started out again, hunting for game. It was still very cold. He began wondering where he could go to get warm. The snow was falling thicker and thicker. Again he stopped under a pine tree, and again he heard a sound.

"This time two holy persons appeared near him. He told them how cold he was and how badly he needed a place

where he could get warm. The holy persons told him to come with them. One walked in front of him and the other walked behind him.

"Soon they came to a mountain, which was a hogan. A blanket was hanging over the door and a rainbow was there, too. The hunter lifted the blanket, but he could not see inside. A holy person told him to move the rainbow. This he did, and he made a fire inside.

"In this place many bears were sleeping. They were all snoring very loudly. When the hunter started the fire the bears woke, and they were angry when they saw the man. 'We don't need any earth people here,'they said. 'Go away.'

"Then a holy person spoke to the bears. 'Don't say that,' he told the bears. 'This man is cold. He needs a place to stay. When you help this poor man, he and other men will help you. They will help you with their prayers and their pollen. They can offer these to you.'

"The bears said the man could stay, but that he must put out the fire. So he put out the fire. Then he asked the bears what could keep other earth people safe if they get lost. The bears told him there were prayers and songs, and they began teaching them to him that very night.

"When daylight came again, the hunter had learned all the prayers and songs. The bears told him the meanings of all the words. They told him that the songs and prayers he learned should be used when one was planning to go on a trip. They said the songs and prayers would protect the traveler on his journey. They also said when someone gets lost or loses something, he should use these songs and prayers and he will find his way or whatever he is looking for.

" 'When you offer prayers with pollen,' the bears told this hunter, 'you must pray at the top of a small hill. The pollen should be put on the tracks of bears at the hill top, especially when the sacred wind blows the most.'

"After they told the young man all these things, they told him to go home. They said they were afraid of the holy people and had to do as those people told them.

"There are many stories like that, my grandson. I will tell you more of them, if you can stay awake a while longer."

Honie took a deep breath and sat up. He was too sleepy for more stories.

The next day Tall Man and Honie went for a walk near Honie's home. Honie took his new bow and arrow with him, hoping his uncle would teach him how to shoot it straight and accurately.

"Do you want to try out your new bow and arrow?" Tall Man asked.

"Yes!" Honie quickly answered.

"What shall we use for a target?" asked Tall Man.

Honie found an old piece of cloth. They used it as a target.

To Honie's surprise, the first arrow he shot went through the cloth. Honie was sure, then, that he would be a good shot with the bow. But, after his first good shot, he missed the target again and again.

Tall Man then showed Honie how best to shoot the arrow. Soon Honie was hitting the target fairly well.

Honie enjoyed the visit of his mother's brother (bida'i) very much. He liked the stories Tall Man told and the lessons he gave.

Tall Man explained that he would have to leave the next day. Honie asked him to come back soon to tell more stories. Tall Man said he would be back as soon as he could.

That night Honie thought about the stories Tall Man had told. Once he awoke in the night. A little glow came from the fire.

"The bears told the hunter to put out the fire," he thought. "I guess they were too warm because of their thick coats. If I'd been the hunter, and had my new bow with me, maybe I'd have shot a bear. No! The bears taught him songs and prayers. I wonder how a bear sings - - - ."

Chapter Three

A Visit and a Request

Two more years passed and Honie continued to grow and to learn. Big Sister had taught him much about caring for the sheep and goats. His father taught him where and how to get firewood and water, and many other things about how to live. His mother's brother told him the stories and sacred ways of the Navahos.

Honie was very happy at his home on Black Mountain. He liked Big Sister very much. He also enjoyed her husband, Redhair. Redhair was pleasant with Honie and they often joked with each other.

Redhair liked to go hunting. Sometimes he took Honie with him. He was a good shot with a bow and arrow. He also had a rifle, but he didn't use it much because he didn't have many bullets.

One spring evening while Honie was gathering firewood that his father had cut, he saw someone coming.

"Father," he called, "I think someone is coming."

"Who is it, Son?" his father asked.

"I don't know," Honie responded.

When the man got closer, Honie's father recognized him as Big Coat, Redhair's father.

"Do you remember Big Coat?" Honie's father asked.

"Yes, I remember him. He was here five years ago when Big Sister and Redhair were married. I was so little then (four years old) that it is hard for me to remember much about him. Why is he coming here?"

"I don't know, Son, but he will tell us later," answered his father.

Honie's father and Big Coat greeted each other with respect. Big Coat explained that he had come to visit and discuss something important.

When Honie took the chopped wood inside, he announced the arrival of Big Coat.

Redhair quickly went to greet his father. They had not seen each other for several months.

Everyone went inside and began visiting. Honie's mother and Big Sister prepared food for the family and their guest.

Big Coat was a large and stately man. Everyone respected him. He was one of the best known medicine men in the area. Big Coat knew four ceremonies: Flintway, Big Starway, Beautyway and the Male Shooting Chant.

Big Coat was a wealthy man. He wore much turquoise and silver jewelry. He also had many head of livestock, but he had only two living children.

Redhair's two older brothers had died during the last two years. Redhair's sister was blind and lived alone with her parents.

"How are things at home?" Redhair asked.

"We had a hard winter, Son. Since your brothers passed away, your mother has had to take care of the sheep most of the time. I often was away performing ceremonies for people who were ill."

He continued, "Your mother is getting old and the work is too hard for her. She needs some help. That is why I came here."

It was clear to everyone what Big Coat was going to ask.

"I was hoping your wife and you might move to our home and care for the livestock. We would build a new hogan for you."

Everyone was silent for a moment. Then Honie's father said that he would call a meeting of all their relatives and discuss this request.

Honie's family and Redhair visited with Big Coat for several hours that night before going to sleep.

Everyone seemed to be happy, but Honie was worried about Big Sister leaving. Big Sister was such a good woman. She knew so much about caring for the sheep and goats. Honie knew he would be lonely without her.

The next day Honie's father sent one of Honie's older brothers to get Little Man, Honie's father's brother. Honie's father then left on horseback for the home of Tall Man. Tall Man lived about 60 miles from Honie's home.

Honie and an older brother went to get Big Man's Brother. Big Man's Brother was the brother of Honie's paternal grandfather (Big Man). When Honie's grandfather died, Big Man's Brother raised Honie's father.

Big Man's Brother controlled most of the land where Honie lived. He was the one who had invited Honie's mother's family to come to Black Mountain. He lived only a few miles from Honie's home.

Big Man's Brother's only daughter and her husband, Black Whiskers, also were invited to attend the meeting. They lived at the same place as Big Man's Brother.

Black Whiskers was a brother of Honie's maternal grandmother. He was the first of Honie's mother's relatives to come to Black Mountain. Shortly after he had married Big Man's Brother's daughter, Big Man's Brother had invited all of Honie's mother's relatives to leave Lukachukai and move to Black Mountain.

Five days after Big Coat arrived, the meeting was held. Two sheep were butchered, and there was plenty to eat for all.

Big Man's Brother took charge of the meeting. Everyone on Black Mountain looked to him as their leader. He had refused to go to Fort Sumner, and he had lived alone with his family on Black Mountain while most other Navahos were at Fort Sumner.

Although Big Man's Brother led the meeting, it was Black Whiskers and Tall Man whose opinions would be given first attention and priority. They were the elders of Big Sister's clan and everyone recognized their position of authority. However, all must agree before a decision could be made.

While the meeting was taking place, Honie herded the sheep with his cousin (bił naa'ash) and Big Sister. His cousin was a son of Little Man. Honie took his bow and arrow with him while herding sheep.

"Will you let me shoot your bow?" Honie's cousin asked.

Honie looked at his cousin. He looked at his bow. He didn't want anyone else shooting it, but this was his cousin, and it would not be polite to refuse him.

"I will let you, when we come to a good open space. You might hit a sheep here," he said.

The other boy took the bow. He held it up and pretended to be shooting with it. Honie wished he would carry it at his side until it was time to use it.

"It will be all right here," Honie said after a while. "I will show you how to shoot."

"I know. I can do it by myself," the older boy said, jerking the bow away when Honie reached for it. "I'm going up on that rock."

Off he ran, with Honie at his heels. When he reached the rock he placed the arrow and let it fly. It arched up and out and went down behind a clump of low bushes.

Both boys leaped off the rock and went to find it. They looked and looked, but there was no sign of it. Honie reached for the bow.

"I'm sorry I lost your arrow," his cousin said. "Maybe you'll find it someday."

Honie was very sad. He was angry, too, but did not show it.

"My uncle gave it to me," Honie said. "He will say our eyes are poor or that it was snatched by something that was afraid we might shoot it. Something - - - -"

At once Honie saw his cousin leap into the air and dash off to the side.

"Snake!" he yelled. "Snake!"

Honie looked where the boy had been walking. There was a snake. A big white-looking snake. It was lying in the grass with its head in the air. It was looking at him.

Honie felt as though his feet were grown to the ground. Big Sister had told him the snakes soon would be coming out of their hiding places into the sun. This was the first one he had seen since last winter's cold weather had set in.

Big Sister had heard the scream, "Snake! Snake!" She came running.

"Where is it?" she called.

Honie's mouth felt dry. His tongue refused to say the words. He pointed.

Big Sister came to his side. She looked at the big snake. Then she laughed.

"He won't hurt you, unless you step on him. Look at the bulge in his middle. He has just swallowed a pack rat or something of about that size. Besides, he is one of the harmless snakes. Don't be so frightened, Honie."

Honie found his voice. He was not frightened now.

"Big Sister," he said, keeping his voice low, "that boy lost my arrow."

"It is just hiding from him," Big Sister said. "It doesn't want him to shoot it any more. We will find it."

"But you might leave soon," Honie said. Tears came into his eyes. "And maybe I can never find it, alone."

"Don't be so sad," Big Sister said, slapping him on the shoulder. "Tomorrow . . . . well, tomorrow I may have some very good news for you, my dear little brother."

Honie wanted to ask what the good news might be, but his cousin came to walk with them, so he did not ask.

Honie had many things to think about that day. He thought about his arrow and wondered if something really had snatched it out of the air and hidden it, for some reason. He thought about Big Sister's promise of good news. He thought of herding the sheep and lambs. He thought of riding behind his uncle on the gray horse. But always he came back to the thought of how lonely he would be herding the sheep without Big Sister.

All at once he realized he was still a small boy who didn't know too much about anything, even sheep, although he'd been around them all his life.

Big Sister had taught him a lot, but there was so much more to be learned. How was he to learn it all without her?

The sheep were grazing contentedly by that time, each ewe with her growing lamb nearby. The sky was blue and cloudless. The sun was hot. The shade was cool.

"How beautiful it all is," Big Sister said. "Look about you, boy. See how lovely our land is. Who would want to live anywhere but here, on our beautiful Black Mountain?"

"Yes, it is beautiful," Honie said. But he thought, "If I only could find my arrow, and if only Big Sister weren't going to leave with Redhair I'd be happier."

"What is that red stuff, growing over there?" the cousin suddenly asked, pointing with his lips to a red spot beside some rocks. "Is it blood?"

"It is a little clump of flowers," Big Sister said. "Many flowers grow here at this time of the season. After a little rain, they come out of the earth and start blooming. The flowers know it soon will be so hot they'll dry up; so they don't wait."

The cousin had run across to see the flowers. He came back with a few blossoms. They were bright yellowish-red and shaped to a point like a brush.

"Paint brushes," Big Sister said, pretending to dip the tip into paint and make designs on Honie's face.

All at once Honie was laughing. The world seemed a better, friendlier place than it had seemed a few minutes before.

The two boys gave war whoops of joy and went prancing and dancing across the meadow like a couple of colts. The dogs and Honie's pet lamb, which he had chosen out of all the spring lambs, raced along with them.

It was on the way home that night that Honie's sharp eyes saw a feather blowing on a bush. It was on the slope beneath the rock from which his cousin had shot the arrow.

Honie said nothing to Big Sister or to his cousin, but he walked quietly over that way to see what the feather was doing on the bush, and what kind of a feather it was. To his keen eyes it looked like an eagle feather.

He was almost afraid to believe he really had found his arrow, but there it was, dangling in the bush, at a place where it easily could have stayed concealed for many years. Before he touched it, Honie noticed how beautifully the black obsidian arrowpoint was finished and how clear the stone was. In his hand, it had looked black. Suspended, as it now was, it was almost clear.

Honie had no pollen with him, but he had learned to be grateful and to say prayers. As he took the arrow from the tree, he thought of a prayer-song:

> "I will say prayers to you, young cedar,
> because you have so gently held my arrow.
> You have held it up for me to find,
> though you could have kept it hidden in the branches.
> Thank you, young cedar. Thank you."

He was still singing his song when he joined Big Sister and his Cousin.

Why are you suddenly so happy?" Big Sister asked.

Honie had been holding the arrow behind him. Now, smiling, he held it up before him.

"The arrow!" Honie's cousin cried. "Good! Now I can try my skill again."

He reached for the arrow and the bow, but Honie held them back.

"No," he said, "it is getting too dark. It would be hard to see, if you were to lose it again. Why don't you ask your grandfather to make you a bow and arrow? He likes to do things for his grandchildren."

The black lamb trotted up and nudged him with its white nose. Honie picked it up in his arms, but it was too heavy for him to carry.

"You're growing up," he told it. "You can walk on your own four feet from now on. Before summer's over you'll be almost grown to full size. I'd look funny trying to carry you then, wouldn't I?"

Big Sister overheard him and laughed.

"Next spring she may be having her first lamb. The way you pet her, she'll probably expect you to carry her and her lamb."

"A man could do it," Honie said, "but I won't be big enough in one year. She'll just have to walk."

Big Sister seemed happy all day. She laughed and talked and made jokes with the boys, but when she closed the corral gate that night she put her head on the top pole and looked sad.

"What has hurt you, Big Sister?" Honie asked.

"These sheep have been my children," she answered. "I have cared for them and held them in my mind all of these years. It is sad to think of leaving them. There will be others, and I'll take good care of them, too, but these sheep are like

relatives. I wish I could take them all along with me to my new home.

Their mother's younger sister would take care of the sheep, however. She lived in the same camp with Honie's family.

Why don't you live here?" Honie asked.

"Because Big Coat and his wife are old. They need their son near them to help with the sheep. They have much land, too, which they want to give to their son and me. It is the best way, but I'll be lonely for Father and Mother and all the others of our family. I'll miss all of you.

Honie slipped his hand into Big Sister's hand. The cousin had run on ahead. They followed, not talking, but caring very much for each other. They understood each other without words.

Before they reached the hogan they could smell meat cooking, and they were hungry after the long day with the sheep.

The meeting had lasted all day. The people seemed to be happy. Honie wondered what had been decided.

"It's time to eat," Honie's mother called.

Everyone got some food and ate heartily. Honie liked the mutton stew, but he kept thinking about Big Sister leaving.

Tall Man announced to Big Sister and Honie that the decision had been made to have Redhair and Big Sister move to Big Coat's home.

Honie's heart sank. Already he felt lonely. He tried to hide his sadness all evening, but Big Sister knew how he felt.

The next day Redhair and Big Sister began to pack. Honie stayed around the hogan while his mother's sister herded the sheep.

By noon all the guests had left. Redhair and Big Sister were not planning to leave until the next day.

That evening Honie was sitting alone near the corral. Big Sister saw him and went to him.

"Little Brother," she said, "I have a surprise for you now."

Honie suddenly remembered that Big Sister had told him that she had a surprise for him.

"What is it?" Honie asked with excitement.

"Redhair and I want you to come with us. We want you to live with us," Big Sister said.

"**Live** with you? **All** the time?" He was almost unable to believe what he had heard.

"Yes, all the time," Redhair said, who had just joined Big Sister and Honie. "There will be no children near us and we have no children of our own. Do you want to come?"

46

"Yes!" Honie replied. "But what will Father and Mother say?"

"It is all right with them," Big Sister answered. "They have given you to me to raise because I have no children of my own."

Honie then talked with his parents about leaving. He was so excited he forgot to think about how much he might miss his parents.

The next morning Big Coat, Redhair, Big Sister and Honie prepared to make the trip to Big Coat's home, which was about 25 miles away.

As they started to leave, Honie's father brought the little black lamb to Honie.

"This little lamb, which has been your pet since her birth, will be the start of your own herd of sheep. Take good care of her. Some day you will have many sheep and goats," his father commented.

"Go in beauty and take care, my children," Honie's mother said tenderly. "May beauty be around you and above you. May you always go in beauty and harmony."

"Haagoonee (Good-bye)," said all of Honie's relatives.

"Baa-a," said the little black lamb.

"She's saying good-bye to her friends," said Big Coat.

"I'm her best friend," Honie said. "I'll keep her from being too lonely at her new home."

He did not know how lonely **he** would be, at first.

Chapter Four

New Home at Long Ridges

It still was light when Honie and the others reached the home of Big Coat, who lived at a place on Black Mountain called Long Ridges (Niinanizaad).

Big Coat's wife was happy to see her husband return with her son and her daughter-in-law (bizha'aad). Big Coat's wife, Woman of Near Water Clan (Asdzaan Tó'ąhaní), had worked hard to care for the sheep and was desperately in need of help.

When Big Coat's wife saw Honie she asked, "Who is this young boy who has come to see us?"

"This is my wife's younger brother. He has come to stay with us," Redhair told his mother.

"Is this the boy who was just this tall when you were married?" Redhair's mother asked.

"Yes," Redhair replied. "He has grown a lot. He soon will be a young man."

"We need a young man here," Redhair's mother commented. " We are happy he has come to stay with us."

Honie liked his new home. Everyone was nice to him. He put his black lamb with the other sheep. The lamb soon adjusted to its new friends.

Shortly after Redhair and the others arrived, there were discussions about where to build a new hogan for Redhair and Big Sister. After a choice was made, Redhair and his father started cutting trees for the new hogan.

The logs had to be pulled by horses to the spot where the new hogan was to be built. Honie helped by leading the horses to the right place. He also helped in other ways as the new hogan was built.

When the hogan was finished and ready to be lived in, the family prepared for the hogan blessing ceremony.

Big Coat directed the ceremony. He took a buckskin pouch of ground white corn from his medicine bag and put the corn in a basket.

Giving the basket of ground corn to Redhair, Big Coat asked Redhair to mark the sides of the hogan — first the east, then the south, then the west and lastly the north, saying ancient prayers of blessing and protection.

The ceremony continued the next day and all that night. There were many beautiful songs.

Honie closed his eyes and listened to the songs which Big Coat sang. They were beautiful. He sang of beauty. He sang of peace and harmony. He sang of Mother Earth and her gifts to men. He sang of the food she supplied for their bodies and of the trees she gave for their hogans.

After the ceremony, Redhair and Big Sister moved into the new hogan. Honie moved in with them. He was very happy. Life was good and beautiful.

Early the next morning, Redhair awakened Honie.

"Come, Little Man," he said. "It's time for our exercise. We must strengthen our lungs and legs. Don't put on much clothing; we will bathe before we come back."

"How far shall we run?" Honie asked, going outside with Redhair.

"Do you see the big tree down the hill? Because this is your first morning, we'll run to the tree. It is close to the spring and the pool."

Redhair was a fast runner. His legs were long and thin and his feet were tough.

Honie ran as fast as he could after Redhair. His feet were not as tough as Redhair's. He felt sharp rocks and sticks and a thorn or so, but he did not stop to look at the soles of his feet. He did not want Redhair to be ashamed of him.

Redhair was waiting for him at the big tree.

"Now we jump into the cold water," he said. "Sometimes it is so cold it makes you yell, but you soon get warm. Are you ready?"

Honie already was shivering in the early morning chill of the mountains, but he said yes.

Redhair jumped into the pool. The water splashed in all directions. He came up, pushing his hair back from his face and spouting water.

Honie jumped in beside him. The water came up over his head. He gasped as he struggled to the surface.

"Good," Redhair cried, his face alight with approval. "You will be a tough man when you grow up. No one will laugh at you . . . . Now, let's run back."

Running brought the blood back to the surface of Honie's skin. He began to feel warm before he even reached the hogan, with its crackling cedar fire.

Redhair and his father had many cattle, mules, donkeys and horses, as well as sheep and goats. They cared for the other livestock, while Big Sister and Honie were busy with the sheep and goats.

The black lamb was growing very rapidly, but she still called to Honie whenever she saw him and came bounding and twisting to meet him.

Honie often sat down and talked to her. He was certain she understood every word he said.

Summer days held their pleasures for Honie. There was much new country for him to explore, under the watchful eye of Big Sister. Sometimes, to his delight, Redhair or Big Coat took him with them.

One day, after the first frost had turned the sumac into beautiful, glowing redness, Big Coat came to Redhair's hogan as Big Sister and Honie prepared to take the sheep to pasture.

"We are going to gather red sumac (chíílchin)," he told Big Sister. "May we take the Little Man (Honie) with us?"

"How can I refuse? It is a part of happy childhood to pick red sumac and eat all one can hold at the same time. Yes, take him with you."

Big Coat's aging wife went with them, riding her horse like a young woman and enjoying the outing."

This time they took a trail about which Honie knew nothing. Everything was strange to him. Down, down, down the trail wound, at first in forest, then in scrubby cedars, then to grassy land.

Below, Honie could see cornfields, with red sumac edging a stream. There were many hogans along the waterway.

"Chíílchinbiitó' " said Big Coat, with a wave of one hand. "Where the red sumac grows beside the water. Would you like to live down here?"

"No," Honie said at once. "I am a Black Mountain boy. I do not want to go away from Black Mountain." And he added, "Even when I get big like Redhair, I want to live on my mountain."

Big Coat chuckled.

"You are a good boy," he said. "I think you should learn the songs and chantways of our people. I think you would be a splendid medicine man someday. Would you like to learn about this work?"

54

"I like the songs," Honie said. "I like to hear you sing. You have such a low, bass voice.

Big Coat was amused, but soon he began singing. His voice ranged from low in his throat to high, thin notes that made little bumps rise on Honie's skin. The boy was almost sorry when they reached the juicy, salty-tasting red sumac berries.

Other Navahos were picking the berries, too. Big Coat knew some of them. They came to him respectfully, recognizing him as a medicine man whose healings always were done in a perfect manner, leaving out none of the ancient prayers and songs.

As they rode back up the mountain, with their sacks of berries, Big Coat stopped singing long enough to say, "Little Man, I think you are old enough to have a horse of your own. I will talk to your father about it."

"Of my own?" Honie said, feeling himself riding in the wind, as he had dreamed so often. "All mine?"

"All yours," Big Coat said. "Every man should have a horse, even if he still is a small man. He is bound to grow, so let him grow, knowing how to handle a horse."

Honie was too happy for words. A horse! What color would it be? A purple-gray with spotted hips, like Redhair's favorite mount? A white horse, like a cloud? A red one, like the horse Big Coat was riding, or an old, slow brown, like the ancient mare Big Coat's wife preferred?

In his mind, Honie chose the gray with dappled hips. He could see it saddled and bridled, its ears pricked up and its eyes alert.

Chapter Five

Father Brings Honie a Gift

The thought of his own horse almost made him forget how much he missed his parents at his new home. He was happy at Long Ridges but he missed his parents and others of his family.

Honie wanted to go back home for a visit but there was no one to go with him. He had hoped his parents might visit him.

His dream came true one evening when he saw his father ride up to the hogan, leading a gentle pinto with a white face which had a black patch over one eye. Honie was very happy to see his father and wondered whose horse his father was leading.

"She is yours," Honie's father said. "You must take care of her, then she will take care of you. Your sister will help you." He smiled and his black eyes twinkled under his heavy black brows. "But don't run races with her for a while. She's too fat for that."

Honie looked at the mare's fat stomach.

"She's going to have a colt, isn't she?" he asked.

"Soon," his father said. "You'll have it to train. By the time you are ready for a young, mettlesome horse it will be old enough for you to ride."

Honie was as happy as he had been the day his uncle brought the bow and arrow. He had no words to tell his father how very happy he felt, but he tried.

"You are kind to me, my father," he said. "You have not forgotten me. I have been lonely for home and my parents. Now you have come to see me and brought me this horse. I am very happy and thankful."

He led the mare in a circle and admired her. Then he got on her and rode her around the area near their hogan.

Honie was disappointed when his father had to leave, but he thought he might go home to visit more often now that he had a horse of his own.

During the next few days, he rode the mare all over Red-hair's grazing area, delighted at the way she responded to his handling of the reins.

He petted her and brushed her with a bundle of stiff grass stems. He was happy to lead or ride her to water and to sit in the shade of a tree while she grazed.

And every morning he raced out to see if, by chance, her colt had been born.

Then came the terrible morning when he found no trace of the mare. Somehow she was gone from the area. He ran to Big Sister.

"She's gone. Someone has taken her," he cried. "Now I have no horse, and I'll not have a little colt to train into a saddlehorse."

"Sh-h! You are no longer a baby," Big Sister reminded him.

Redhair already had gone to see that his cattle and horses were on their range, so Big Sister went to the hogan of Big Coat and his wife and told them about what happened.

"See if you can pick up her tracks, while I saddle my horse. She was born in the canyon of the spouting water, down below. Perhaps she has gone back there to give birth to her colt," the old man said.

Big Sister and Honie criss-crossed the area. There were many tracks of sheep and horses, but the mare's track would be easy to see because she had one split hoof. Soon Honie cried out, "Here they are. Her tracks. They lead down the mountain."

He rode behind Big Coat on the horse with the spotted hips, and before noon they found the pinto mare, near the artesian spring.

She was lying down when they first saw her, but she got up and whinnied a soft welcome. Then she nudged a little curled-up object that had been lying beside her. It was her newborn colt, a knobby-kneed, spraddle-legged little pinto, with a black face and a white patch over one eye

Honie began laughing.

"So here you are, Runs-Away," he said, giving the mare a name. "And here's your son, White-Patch-On-Eye, who looks a little like my black lamb."

From then on, Honie had a new interest. He almost forgot the black lamb, and it gradually stopped running to him, as it had for months.

Sometimes he called to it, just to see it lift its head and answer with a friendly "baa-a-a."

By the time the golden autumn days were gone and the cold winds of winter began to blow, the colt was sleek and fat and as frisky as any colt could be. He followed his mother wherever Big Sister or Honie rode her, nosing curiously into bushes, or lying lazily in some sheltered, sunny place, just enjoying himself and growing.

One day while Big Sister and Honie were herding the sheep a storm suddenly appeared. The wind blew hard. Honie's colt found some shelter near a rocky ridge.

Honie, like his colt, went to some large rocks for shelter and was preparing to test his skill with the bow and arrow when a movement in a tree caught his eye. At the same moment two crows flew over cawing loudly.

The movement, and the crow flights, alerted Honie. Poised, ready to send the arrow toward its target, he glanced at the tree over which the crows cawed.

What he saw sent a chill through him. For an instant he was shocked to stillness. Then he faced the danger and knew what he must do.

Beneath that tree, stretched lazily on the grass, lay his beloved colt. Above it, creeping out onto a thick branch, was a wildcat.

Honie knew what was about to happen. The cat would spring down upon the sleeping colt, sink its fangs into the colt's throat and end its beautiful life.

He had to stop it. His feathered arrow must wing true.

"Tree-protected-arrow," he prayed, taking careful aim, "let the eagle feather guide you."

"Shoot straight, Little Hunter," his uncle had said, and this he must do, if his colt were to live.

The arrow winged away through the still air. The wild-cat, intent on his prey, crept an inch closer, then the sharp obsidian point punctured his spotted skin and buried itself in his vital organs.

With an ear-piercing cry of agony and anger, the cat sprang to the ground. It landed in a rolling, spitting, hissing

ball, its feet clawing at the arrow, snapping the shaft and shredding the feathers.

Honie gave a great shout, dropped his bow and jumped from the rocks. As he ran toward the thrashing, squalling cat, he picked up a heavy rock, intending to crush the cat's head with it.

Big Sister had heard the noise. She turned the pinto mare and came galloping to Honie's aid.

"Be careful, Little Brother," she screamed. "Don't get too close to him. Watch out for his claws."

Honie was dancing around the agonized cat, trying to get in a position for hurling the rock. He had just raised his arm to deliver the blow when the cat became aware of him. For one instant the blazing yellow eyes met his furious gaze, then the cat hurled itself at the boy.

Honie's rock hit it just as it slashed him from thigh to knee with its claws. It quivered and lay still, and Honie stood looking down at it, panting and shaking.

"Are you hurt, Little Brother?" Big Sister cried, sliding from her pony and running to his side. "Oh! You **are** hurt. Get on the horse. Go to Big Coat at once. He will know what to do about your clawed places."

Honie looked down. He had not known that he was hurt. He saw blood running down his leg and felt the first burning sensation in the wounds. It was the first time he had ever been badly hurt.

"Hurry! Take the mare and go. **At once!**" Big Sister urged him.

He made no answer. Suddenly he was feeling very sick inside. Later, he didn't remember getting on the mare or riding back to Big Coat's hogan. He didn't remember Big Coat taking him from the horse and carrying him inside.

The next thing he remembered was lying on a sandpainting, while Big Coat performed his services as a medicine man. Big Coat had cared for the wounds and now was singing the songs of Lifeway.

In Honie's fevered state he thought the shadows dancing on the hogan walls were wild animals: wildcats, bears, mountain lions, wolves and coyotes.

After a time, he realized his own mother and father were in the hogan. Redhair and Big Sister also were there.

"Everything must be done right," Big Coat urged. "This is a very sick boy. The cat's poisons are working fast. We must pray them out of him or they will kill him."

Honie heard the words and knew that he did not want to die. He wanted to live. He wanted to train his pinto colt, when it was old enough. He wanted to learn to shoot a rifle, like Redhair's. He wanted to keep on living on his beloved Black Mountain.

Big Coat sang songs. He sang them low and gently, he sang them strongly and loud. The sound was soothing. The heat was going out of Honie's body. He sighed once, softly, and went to sleep.

He did not hear Big Coat say, "He will live."

Chapter Six

Becoming a Man

Lambs and colts and boys grow rapidly.

After his experience with the wildcat, Honie seemed to change. He no longer was a little boy. His legs were long and strong. He was lean and tough. He could run with Redhair and almost keep up with him, in spite of Redhair's longer legs.

He no longer played little boys' games. Instead, he busied himself with learning new skills. Tall Man, his mother's brother, sometimes came over and stayed for days, sitting by the fire during the evening hours and teaching Honie to make quirts, bull whips and belts from braided rawhide, or showing him how to dye horsehair and braid it into beautifully patterned hatbands.

One day he brought some tanned elk hide and said, "Every man should be able to make his own moccasins. It is time you had lessons in this craft. Someday you may have many in your family and you will need to know how to keep them comfortable. Bruised feet add years before they come."

Honie still had the bow his uncle made for him, but it hung on the wall. He no longer played with it. Instead, soon after he killed the wildcat, Redhair came home from a trip to a distant trading post and handed Honie a small rifle. He quickly became a good shot and brought home game for the daily meals.

His greatest treasures were the strand of turquoise beads, which Big Coat had given him, and the black obsidian arrowhead which he had removed from the dead wildcat. He kept the point in a little bag, made of doeskin, which he hung on the hogan wall beside the bow.

These were relics of his boyhood. Now he was growing rapidly toward young manhood and his treasures were the twin lambs the black ewe had given birth to in the spring, and the yearling colt with which he was working daily.

White-Patch-On-Eye liked to pretend he was afraid of Honie. When Honie tried to slip the bridle on him he snorted like a wild horse and danced away.

But Honie was patient. Little by little he won the colt's confidence. Soon he could put his arms around the proudly

arched neck. Then he taught it to lead behind its mother. There came a day, when the colt was a two-year-old, when Honie tied a saddleblanket on it.

This the colt did not like. It kicked and bucked until the blanket slipped beneath it and fell to the ground. But Honie kept putting it back on, until at last the colt accepted it.

"Better not try to ride him, yet," Redhair advised. "He has a lot of spirit. I think that when he feels your weight he will explode with fright and throw you off."

It was good advice, but one day Honie could not resist bridling the colt and slipping onto his back. For a moment the colt stood still, wondering what to do with that strange new weight that clung to him with gripping knees. Then, in about three bucking jumps, he shook Honie loose and threw him in the dirt.

That was the first time Honie was thrown, but not the last, before he gentled Patch enough for riding. Even then the spirited pony often delighted in pretending he was going to go back to his old wild ways.

When Honie was accustomed to the saddle, and Patch no longer tried his best to throw him, Redhair took Honie with him to round up the cattle. They had strayed in many directions and Redhair hired two other boys to help. One of them was the older cousin who had shot Honie's arrow into the trees during the meeting to decide whether Redhair and Big Sister would move to Long Ridges.

Honie could be spared now, for Big Sister had brought their younger sister to her home to help her. Big Sister had

no children of her own, so she was happy to help her mother raise the little ones of the family.

Honie liked riding after the cattle and helping to herd the many fine horses owned by Redhair and Big Coat. It was a man's work, and he was fast growing into a real man. Sometimes Honie's father would have Honie come back home and help with the cattle there.

"Someday you will have livestock of your own to care for," his father told him. "We will choose a girl for you to marry. She might have many livestock, and you will help her care for them. You also will get some of your mother's and my livestock."

"I don't want to get married," Honie declared.

"Maybe not, now," his father said, jogging along beside Honie on his big, powerful saddlehorse. "But you will. It is the responsibility of Tall Man and me to find a girl for you and to arrange your marriage."

Honie felt a little embarrassed. He did not like the subject of marriage.

"You don't mean very soon, do you, Father?" Honie asked.

"Don't be so frightened . . . . No, not today. But the years go rapidly. Your cousin, for instance, is two years older than you are and already his father has a girl picked out for him."

Honie thought about his talk with his father as he rode back to Redhair's home after his work with his father had been completed.

One day Redhair's mother went to gather piñon nuts and did not come back. They found her, sitting beside a tree with her hands folded in her lap, as though she simply had become tired and had sat down to rest.

Big Coat mourned the death of his wife. They had lived together for many years in harmony. His hogan no longer seemed like home and he came more and more often to the hogan of his son for comfort and for good food.

"Come live in my home with me," Big Coat said to Honie one day. "You are a young man now, and old enough to begin to learn the songs and prayers and the ancient chantways of our people. I will teach you all I know. I will show you all the holy places."

He turned to Redhair and Big Sister.

"It would be a credit to you to have a younger brother who is learning to be a medicine man. Will you release him to me for the remainder of my few years?"

They sat in silence for a long time, thinking over this proposal. Redhair was the first to speak. "Do you wish to do this?" he asked Honie.

"I'd like to learn. I'd like to help Grandfather (as he called Big Coat) with his ceremonies," Honie said. "But there is a lot to learn. I don't know that I'd be able to learn everything, but I would try, if you don't need me."

"I think he should be allowed to try," Big Sister said. "It is good to be a medicine man, but only those who truly want to do this work should try it, I think. I am not sure my brother will become a medicine man, yet learning the songs and prayers and chants will be of use to him all his life."

"I need you," Redhair said. "I have no son of my own. But I will not hold you. My father wanted me to learn the work he does, but I wanted to ride after my cattle and my horses. I wanted to see my livestock increase, as it has. The life of a medicine man is not an easy one. My father has gone to heal people in the middle of winter. He has gone in snowstorms and in rainstorms and in raging dust storms. He always has given thought to others before he thought of himself. Do you think you can follow in his footsteps?"

73

"I don't know," Honie said honestly, "but I can try."

Big Coat was a strict teacher. He would not allow Honie to practice shooting or to go horseback riding until he had sung the songs for hours and listened to long explanations of their meanings.

"Things must be done right," Big Coat kept insisting. "To do them wrong is to undo them. They are only helpful when done right."

After many weeks of this constant teaching, Honie was glad when the old man said, "Now, we will take a long journey on horseback to some of the holy places."

It was a bright October day when they started. The sun was warm, the winds had gone to sleep and a few little fluffy clouds floated lazily in the blue sky.

"Where will we go first?" Honie asked.

"To the canyon. To the beautiful Canyon de Chelly with its bright walls and smooth floor," the old man said, smiling as he mounted his horse.

As they rode, Big Coat told Honie about many holy places.

"I did not go to Fort Sumner with the others," the old man said. "But many of my relatives went. When they were set free and allowed to come home, it was to the holy places they went first. . . Do you have the bag of pollen I gave you? And the white ground corn?"

Honie patted the two leather pouches that hung at his belt.

"Yes, Grandfather, I have pollen and cornmeal, too."

"It is good. We will visit many places and offer much pollen and cornmeal and many prayers. I have not done this for many years. It will make me happy and it will teach you things you should know when you become a medicine man."

"I may not be a good medicine man," Honie said. "Have you noticed that I do not learn all the songs with ease? Sometimes I say the wrong words. It worries me. Perhaps you should be teaching someone else.

"The best singers sometimes are slow in learning," Big Coat said, but he looked grave and sad. "I should have taught someone years ago, but when one is younger it seems that he never will grow old," he sighed. "We are all a little slow in learning the things that make up a lifetime."

Honie was sorry he had made the old man sad. He tried to tell a joke, and when Big Coat failed to see anything funny in it, he began singing. After a moment Big Coat joined him, tapping on his saddle pommel as though it were a drum. They came singing to the mouth of the canyon.

"In this canyon," Big Coat said, "The people hid. And, in this canyon, they were discovered by the soldiers and killed. Men, women and children were killed. Their stores of corn and dried meat were destroyed. Their beautiful peach trees were cut down. They fought with great courage and strength, but they were badly outnumbered.

"Some of them never surrendered, and many of them came back. This trip will honor them. This trip will be in memory of them and their bravery. Think of them as we ride. Think of them walking the long way to that foreign place. Think of them waiting and waiting to come home. Many of them died while they waited. Many of them were broken-hearted, seeing their old people and their babies die and pass from life."

"But you did not suffer those things," Honie said gently. "Black Mountain hid and sheltered you. Don't let them hurt you so much now. They are of the past."

The old man seemed not to hear him.

"Ah, here is the first of the holy places I will show you. Others have been here. I can see they have added their

75

blessings of meal here at the beginning of the trail to the cave. Let us tie our horses here, in this little grove, and walk up to the cave.

Honie noticed how bent and tired the old medicine man suddenly seemed as he let himself down carefully from his horse and hobbled over to tie it to a sapling.

"We will offer our prayers here," the old man panted, "for this is a holy place. They say there's a moaning sound in it, when it storms . . . Listen! Do you hear it."

"No, Grandfather," Honie said. "Please sit down and rest. You look tired."

"Yes, Grandson. I am tired. And I have pain in here."
He touched his left side. "But I must give the pollen first.
The pollen is sacred, you know, and the basis of all life.
Always carry pollen with you, so that supernatural beings
will recognize you as a human."

"Yes, Grandfather," Honie said respectfully, and he
took the old man's arm to help him the last few feet up the
cliff wall.

Big Coat made his prayers and sprinkled the pollen; then
he turned to go back down the cliff, but he was shaking
badly.

"Look across the canyon," he said. "There is one of the
places where the people tried to hide from the soldiers. They
were shot. Some of them fell to the bottom of the canyon and
were broken like clay jugs . . . . Somewhere near here there's
a place where frogs used to live . . . . Or did we already visit
that place?"

He sat down, struggling for breath, and Honie looked
at him in alarm. This trip was not a happy one. It had started
well, but something was dreadfully wrong with Big Coat.
There was a strange look in his eyes. A look of pain and
fear.

"Grandfather, we must start home," Honie said. "It is
a beautiful canyon, as you told me, but your son will worry
about you. So will my sister. You wouldn't want them to
worry, would you?"

"Worry? About us? No, but there's another place. I
don't remember just where it is . . . . I think we called it
'Home of Eagles' . . ."

He got up and staggered down the trail. Once he stopped
and put his hand to his head, looking around as though he
were lost.

"Sit down, Grandfather, and I'll bring the horses over
here," Honie said. "I think you are not feeling well."

"You are a good boy," the old man quavered, sitting down, as Honie had urged him.

Honie helped him into the saddle, but before they had gone far on the homeward trail, Honie knew the old man could not stay in the saddle the whole day. He dismounted, got onto Big Coat's horse and held him the rest of the way. Honie led Patch.

Redhair saw them coming. He came to help carry his father to his own hogan and put him to bed. He went to sleep at once. During the night he wakened a few times and talked about holy places, frogs and spouting water; then he was still.

"He was a good man," his son said. "He lived a good life."

After Big Coat's death Honie had less to do. There was no one to teach him the ceremonies. Redhair had married

Honie's younger sister a few years earlier, and now he had two children from his second wife.

Big Sister was raising one of the children, so both Redhair and Big Sister now had children to live with and raise.

Honie was no longer a child. He was sixteen years old and a young man. Honie realized that his place no longer should be with Big Sister. His father and mother's brother had chosen a girl for him, and they were planning soon to propose the marriage.

Honie was now ready to marry and take on the responsibilities of manhood. As he thought about the changes occurring in his life, Honie remembered what Big Sister had told him about growing up: "All things grow and get older. Even you, Little Brother, soon will be a man."

He was tall. As tall as Redhair and taller than his own father. And he was strong and quick, a good rider and a good shot with a rifle.

He had learned much from everyone, especially from Big Sister, Tall Man, his father, Redhair and Big Coat. But there was much yet to be learned, especially the traditions of his people. The legends were sometimes funny and sometimes sad. The songs held much of the past in their words.

And there would be the future. It would hold mysteries he would have to solve. But that was as it should be. That was a way of growing.

Suddenly memories began sweeping through his mind. He thought of the first day he went out with Big Sister to herd the sheep, and of how happy he was. He thought of the day his cousin lost the arrow and how the cedar had held it up for him to find. He thought of the terrible fright the wildcat had given him and of the sickness he had suffered because of its claws, and of Big Coat's healing chants and Tall Man's stories.

Truly Black Mountain was his home and the earth his mother. As long as he could live in his beautiful Navaholand life would be good.

As he walked back toward the hogan he began singing. It was the song he had made up for the cedar tree so long before, but it was also a prayer for his home and all those dear to him.

"I will sing my prayers to you, young cedar," he hummed. "because you have so gently held my arrow - - -"

Big Sister came to the door of the hogan and stood watching the tall boy walking toward her. Redhair had gathered an armful of wood for the hogan fire.

"Why are you smiling?" Big Sister asked as he came near.

"Has something made you happy, Tall Boy?"

"Yes," Honie said. "The mountain makes me happy. The earth makes me happy. My people make me happy. My horse and my sheep make me happy. I am becoming a man."